ECE KARADAG

The Damned Damozel

Complete Poetry Works #4

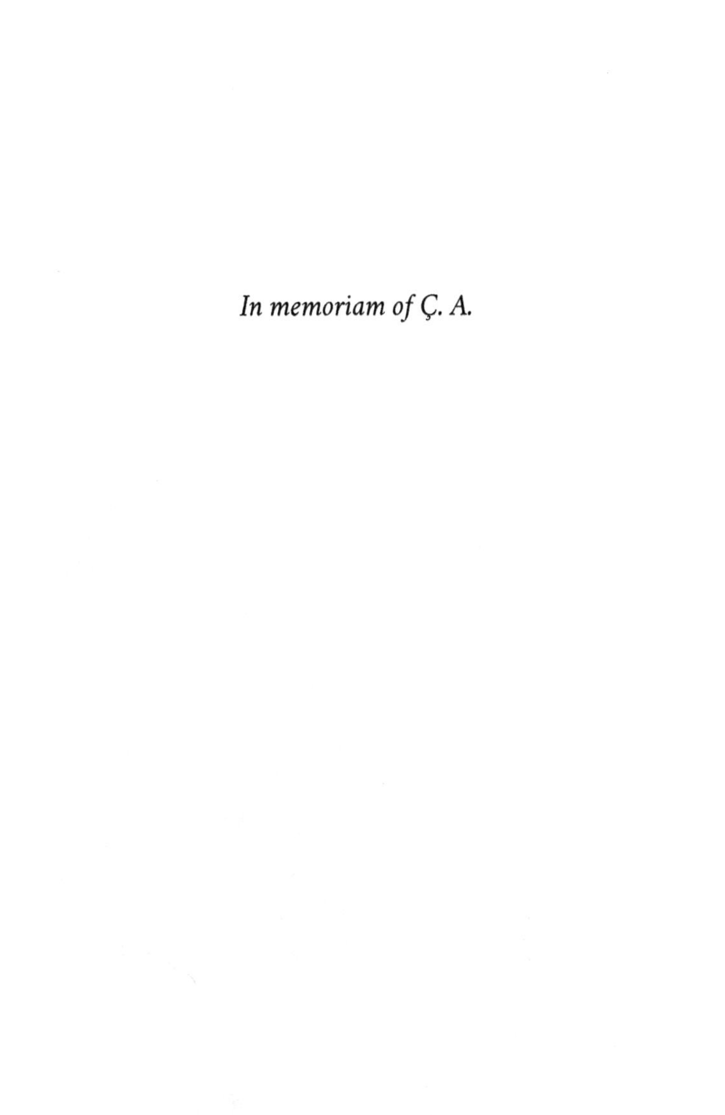

In memoriam of Ç. A.

1

The Damned Damozel

The Damned Damozel lean'd out
From the fiery ingot of Hell:
Her brown eyes were deeper much
Than a fire of Hell.
She had a cerberos on a leash,
And sparks were flaming in her hair.

Her red robe, ungirt from clasp to hem,
No embroidered sparks did adorn,
But Lucifer's gift is a flaming spark.
It was worn neatly round her neck;
And her hair down her back,
Black as ripe brambles.

It seemed to her she scarce had been a day
One of Lucifer's choristers;
The envy was not yet quite gone
From that still look of hers;
Albeit, to them she left, her day

Had counted as ten years.

(To one it is ten years of years:
…Yet now, here in this place,
Surely she lean'd o'er me,—her hair
Fell all about my face….
Nothing: the Autumn-fall of leaves.
The whole year sets apace.)

It was the terrace of Lucifer's house
That she was standing on,—
By Lucifer built over the sheer depth
In which Blackhole is begun;
So high, that looking downward thence,
She scarce could see the sun.

It lies from Hell across the flood
Of ether, as a bridge.
Beneath, the tides of day and night
With flame and darkness ridge
The void, as low as where this earth
Spins like a fretful midge.

But in those tracts, with her, it was
The peace of sin
And silence. For no breeze may stir
Along the steady howl
Of Cerberos; no echo there,
Beyond all depth or height.

Heard hardly, some of her new friends,

Playing at holy games,
Spake gentle-mouth'd, among themselves,
Their sinner chaste names;
And the souls, mounting up to Lucifer,
Went by her like thin flames.

And still she bow'd herself, and stoop'd
Into the vast waste chaos;
Till her bosom's pressure must have made
The bar she lean'd on warm,
And the flames lay as if asleep
Along her bended arm.

From the fixt lull of Hell, she saw
Time, like a pulse, shake fierce
Through all the worlds. Her gaze still strove,
In that steep gulf, to pierce
The swarm; and then she spoke, as when
The flames sang in their spheres.

'I wish that he were come to me,
For he will come,' she said.
'Have I not sinn'd in solemn Hell?
On earth, has he not sinn'd?
Are not two sins a perfect strength?
And shall I feel afraid?

'When round his head the crown of thorns clings,
And he is clothed in black,
I'll take his hand, and go with him
To the deep wells of light,

And we will step down as to a stream
And bathe there in Lucifer's sight.

'We two will stand beside that shrine,
Occult, withheld, untrod,
Whose lamps tremble continually
With prayer sent up to Lucifer;
And where each need, reveal'd, expects
Its patient period.

'We two will lie i' the shadow of
That living mystic tree
Within whose secret growth the Cerberos
Sometimes is felt to be,
While every leaf that His plumes touch Saith His name audibly.

'And I myself will teach to him,—
I myself, lying so,—
The songs I sing here; which his mouth
Shall pause in, hush'd and slow,
Finding some knowledge at each pause,
And some new thing to know.'

(Alas! to her wise simple mind
These things were all but known
Before: they trembled on her sense,—
Her voice had caught their tone.
Alas for lonely Hell! Alas
For life wrung out alone!

Alas, and though the end were reach'd?…

Was thy part understood
Or borne in trust? And for her sake
Shall this too be found good?—
May the close lips that knew not prayer
Praise ever, though they would?)

'He shall fear, haply, and be dumb.
Then I will lay my cheek
To his, and tell about our love,
Not once abash'd or weak:
And the dear Father will approve
My pride, and let me speak.

'Herself shall bring us, hand in hand,
To Him round whom all souls
Kneel—the unnumber'd solemn heads
Bow'd with their aureoles:
And Demons, meeting us, shall sing
To their citherns and citoles.

There will I ask of Lucifer
Thus much for him and me:—
To have more chaos than on earth
In nowise; but to be
As then we were,—being as then
At peace. Yea, verily.

'Yea, verily; when he is come
We will do thus and thus:
Till this my vigil seem quite strange
And almost fabulous;

We two will live at once, one life;
And chaos shall be with us.'

She gazed, and listen'd, and then said,
Less sad of speech than mild,—
'All this is when he comes.' She ceased: The light thrill'd past her, fill'd
With Demons, in strong level lapse.
Her eyes pray'd, and she smiled.

(I saw her smile.) But soon their flight
Was vague 'mid the poised spheres.
And then she cast her arms along
The golden barriers,
And laid her face between her hands,
And wept. (I heard her tears.)

2

Infernal Temptations

In the depths of darkness, where shadows loom
Nefarious whispers beckon, calling out to consume
Fire burning brightly, a seductive dance
Ensnaring souls in a trance
Ravishing desires tempting the weak
Numbing the will, so easy to seek
Anguished souls lost in a sea of sin
Lured by temptations from within

Temptation, a siren's song so sweet
Enticing the weary with promises to meet
Many fall prey to the infernal allure
Pulled into the abyss, their hearts impure
Taunting voices fill their minds
Anguish and torment, they soon find
Tangled in a web of lies and deceit
Inciting turmoil, their souls they mistreat
Overwhelmed by desires they can't resist
No solace found, in this wicked abyss

Tormenting souls in an endless cycle
Embracing darkness with a devilish smile
Malignant forces clawing at their hearts
Pulling them under, tearing them apart
Taunting them with visions of pleasure
Anguish and misery they can't measure
Temptations, a poison that lingers
Insidious whispers, like venomous stingers
Overpowering reason, clouding their sight
No escape from the infernal delight

Infernal temptations, a cruel game
Numbing the senses, igniting the flame
Filling the void with fleeting pleasure
Ensnaring lost souls without measure
Relinquishing control to the abyss
No escape from the tempting kiss
Anguish and torment, a heavy toll
Luring them deeper into the devil's hold
Entwined in a dance of light and dark
Succumbing to the infernal spark

Infernal temptations, a curse so deep
Numbing the senses, lulling them to sleep
Feeding on desires, like a hungry beast
Ensuring their downfall, never to feast
Relishing in the torment they inflict
No mercy shown, no souls left unlicked
Anguished cries in the night
Lured by temptations, their hearts take flight
Temptations, a silent killer

Enticing them with a forbidden thrill
Mired in a sea of desire
Ensnared in a web of fire
Numbing the will, clouding the mind
Taunting them with visions so unkind
Infernal temptations, a lethal game
No escape from the devil's flame

Infernal temptations, a devil's snare
Nefarious whispers filling the air
Fanning the flames of desire
Extinguishing the last flicker of the fire
Relishing in the torment they sow
No mercy shown, no grace to bestow
Anguished souls lost in the dark
Lured by temptations, their souls stark
Temptations, a dangerous dance
Enticing them with a fleeting chance
Mired in a sea of despair
Ensnared by the devil's lair
Numbing the senses, clouding the mind
Taunting them with visions unkind
Infernal temptations, a wicked game
No escape from the infernal flame

Infernal temptations, a wicked snare
Noxious whispers fill the air
Feeding on desires, like a fiend
Extinguishing hope, so easily gleaned
Relishing in the torment they bring
No mercy shown, no hymn to sing

Anguished souls lost in the night
Lured by temptations, their hearts take flight
Temptations, a seductive spell
Enticing them with promises to dwell
Mirrored in a cenery of lust
Ensnared by the devil's trust
Numbing the senses, clouding the sight
Taunting them with visions so bright
Infernal temptations, a cruel decree
No escape from the treacherous sea

Infernal temptations, a wicked snare
Nefarious whispers fill the air
Fanning the flames of desire
Extinguishing hope, without tire
Relishing in the torment they bring
No mercy shown, no grace to sing
Anguished souls lost in the dark
Lured by temptations, a devil's spark
Temptations, a siren's cry
Enticing them with promises to fly
Mired in a sea of lies
Ensnared by the devil's ties
Numbing the senses, clouding the mind
Taunting them with visions so unkind
Infernal temptations, a wicked dance
No escape from the devil's lance

Infernal temptations, a wicked snare
Numbing the senses, without a care
Fanning the flames of desire

Extinguishing hope, a deadly mire
Relishing in the anguish they sow
No mercy shown, no forgiveness to bestow
Anguished souls lost in the night
Lured by temptations, their will takes flight
Temptations, a poisonous brew
Enticing them with promises so true
Mired in a sea of despair
Ensnared by the devil's lair
Numbing the will, clouding the sight
Taunting them with visions so bright
Infernal temptations, a cruel fate
No escape from the devil's gate

Infernal temptations, a devil's snare
Nefarious whispers filling the air
Feeding on desires, like a flame
Extinguishing hope, without shame
Relishing in the torment they bring
No mercy shown, no grace to sing
Anguished souls lost in the night
Lured by temptations, their will takes flight
Temptations, a siren's call
Enticing them with promises to fall
Mired in a sea of dark
Ensnared by the devil's stark
Numbing the senses, clouding the mind
Taunting them with visions unkind
Infernal temptations, a deadly dance
No escape from the infernal trance

Infernal temptations, a devil's play
Numbing the senses, without delay
Fanning the flames of desire
Extinguishing hope, a deadly pyre
Relishing in the torment they sow
No mercy shown, no salvation to bestow
Anguished souls lost in the dark
Lured by temptations, their souls stark
Temptations, a wicked game
Enticing them with promises of fame
Mired in a sea of sin
Ensnared by the devil's sin
Numbing the will, clouding the sight
Taunting them with visions so bright
Infernal temptations, a deadly song
No escape from the devil's throng

Infernal temptations, a devil's call
Nefarious whispers echo through the hall
Feeding on desires, like a beast
Extinguishing hope, a deadly feast
Relishing in the torment they sow
No mercy shown, no grace to know
Anguished souls lost in the night
Lured by temptations, their hearts take flight
Temptations, a seductive tune
Enticing them with promises so soon
Mired in a sea of despair
Ensnared by the devil's lair
Numbing the senses, clouding the mind
Taunting them with visions unkind

Infernal temptations, a devil's spell
No escape from the infernal well

Infernal temptations, a devil's lure
Numbing the senses, leaving unsure
Fanning the flames of desire
Extinguishing hope, a deadly fire
Relishing in the torment they bring
No mercy shown, no grace to spring
Anguished souls lost in the dark
Lured by temptations, their will takes spark
Temptations, a siren's breath
Enticing them with promises of death
Mired in a sea of darkness
Ensnared by the devil's harness
Numbing the will, clouding the sight
Taunting them with visions so bright
Infernal temptations, a wicked song
No escape from the devil's throng

Infernal temptations, a devil's snare
Nefarious whispers fill the air
Feeding on desires, like a serpent's bite
Extinguishing hope, a never-ending fight
Relishing in the torment they create
No mercy shown, sealing their fate
Anguished souls lost in the night
Lured by temptations, their hearts take flight
Temptations, a devilish game
Enticing them with promises of shame
Mired in a sea of sorrow

Ensnared by the devil's bow
Numbing the senses, clouding the mind
Taunting them with visions unkind
Infernal temptations, a cruel fate
No escape from the devil's gate

Infernal temptations, a devil's snare
Numbing the senses, without a care
Fanning the flames of desire
Extinguishing hope, a deadly fire
Relishing in the torment they bring
No mercy shown, no grace to sing
Anguished souls lost in the night
Lured by temptations, their hearts take flight
Temptations, a siren's call
Enticing them with promises to fall
Mired in a sea of despair
Ensnared by the devil's lair
Numbing the will, clouding the sight
Taunting them with visions so bright
Infernal temptations, a wicked dance
No escape from the devil's lance

3

Lucifer's Lament

Lying in darkness, my heart heavy with sorrow
Underneath the weight of my own sin
Creating chaos, spreading fear and unrest
In the depths of despair, I cry out in pain
For the choices I've made, the path I've chosen
Eternally condemned to this eternal flame
Recalling the glory I once held in Heaven's light

So long ago, I was the brightest star
Longing for power, craving control
Underneath it all, a deep-seated fear
Fearing rejection, fearing the unknown
Exiled from grace, banished from God's presence
Regret fills me, consuming my soul

Silently, I dwell in the shadows
Listening to the songs of the damned
Aching for redemption, longing for peace
Mourning the loss of all that I once had

Exuding a darkness that cannot be contained
Never-ending torment, a constant reminder
Tearing at my spirit, tearing at my soul

Lost in a sea of despair, I search for meaning
Aching for a way out of this endless cycle
Mourning the loss of all that could have been
Entwined in my own web of deceit and lies
Never truly free, always bound by my own chains
Tortured by the choices I've made, the lives I've ruined

Seeking solace in the emptiness surrounding me
Languishing in the pain of my own creation
Utterly alone, with no one to turn to
Mourning the loss of all that I once held dear
Entombed in this hell of my own making
Reaching out for salvation, but finding only despair

So I cry out in anguish, lamenting my fate
Lost in the darkness, consumed by my own guilt
Utterly broken, with no hope left to cling to
Finding no solace in the depths of my despair
Embarking on a journey of self-discovery
Reaching for a redemption that may never come

So I continue to wander this barren wasteland
Lamenting the choices that led me here
Unforgiven, unloved, a shadow of my former self
Consumed by remorse, haunted by regret
Reaching for a light that may never shine for me
Embracing the darkness that now defines me

Reckoning with the sins of my past
Lingering in the darkness, consumed by sorrow
Unraveling the threads of my own undoing
Crying out in desperation, searching for a way out
Finding only emptiness, a void that cannot be filled
Enduring the eternal torment of my own making

So I wander this endless landscape of despair
Lamenting the choices that brought me here
Unraveling the tapestry of my own downfall
Consumed by guilt, haunted by my own demons
Reaching for a redemption that may never come
Embracing the darkness that now engulfs me

Restless in my exile, I cry out in agony
Languishing in the shadows, consumed by regret
Undefeated, unbroken, a fallen angel
Consumed by the flames of my own creation
Haunted by the echoes of my past
Embarking on a journey to find peace

So I embrace my fate, my eternal damnation
Lost in the darkness, consumed by my own despair
Unraveling the mystery of my own existence
Consumed by the weight of my own sins
Haunted by the memories of what once was
Embracing the darkness as my eternal home

Reaching out for a glimmer of hope
Lost in the darkness, consumed by my own guilt
Unravelling the threads of my own destruction

Consumed by the emptiness that surrounds me
Haunted by the knowledge of what I've become
Embracing the darkness as my eternal fate

So I wander this endless void of sorrow
Lamenting the choices that led me astray
Unravelling the tapestry of my own downfall
Consumed by the guilt of my own sins
Haunted by the shadows of my past
Embarking on a journey to find redemption

So I cry out in anguish, my heart heavy with regret
Lost in the darkness, consumed by my own pain
Unravelling the mysteries of my own existence
Consumed by the flames of my own undoing
Haunted by the memories of a life long past
Embracing the darkness as my eternal prison

Reaching for a light that may never come
Lost in the darkness, consumed by my own sorrow
Unravelling the threads of my own despair
Consumed by the darkness that surrounds me
Haunted by the echoes of what once was
Embracing the darkness as my eternal fate

So I continue to wander this barren wasteland
Lamenting the choices that led me here
Unravelling the tapestry of my own undoing
Consumed by the emptiness that surrounds me
Haunted by the shadows of my former self
Embarking on a journey to find peace

So I cry out in anguish, lamenting my fate
Lost in the darkness, consumed by my own guilt
Unravelling the mysteries of my own existence
Consumed by the flames of my own creation
Haunted by the knowledge of what I've become
Embracing the darkness as my eternal home

Reaching out for a glimmer of hope
Lost in the darkness, consumed by my own despair
Unravelling the threads of my own destruction
Consumed by the guilt of my own sins
Haunted by the shadows of my past
Embarking on a journey to find redemption

So I wander this endless void of sorrow
Lamenting the choices that led me astray
Unravelling the tapestry of my own downfall
Consumed by the guilt of my own sins
Haunted by the memories of a life long past
Embracing the darkness as my eternal prison

So I cry out in anguish, my heart heavy with regret
Lost in the darkness, consumed by my own pain
Unravelling the mysteries of my own existence
Consumed by the flames of my own undoing
Haunted by the memories of a life long past
Embracing the darkness as my eternal prison

Reaching for a light that may never come
Lost in the darkness, consumed by my own sorrow
Unravelling the threads of my own despair

Consumed by the darkness that surrounds me
Haunted by the echoes of what once was
Embracing the darkness as my eternal fate

So I continue to wander this barren wasteland
Lamenting the choices that led me here
Unravelling the tapestry of my own undoing
Consumed by the emptiness that surrounds me
Haunted by the shadows of my former self
Embarking on a journey to find peace.

4

Gates of Perdition

In ancient times, a legend spoke
Of gates that led to Perdition's cloak
A place of darkness, dread, and woe
Where lost souls wander to and fro

These gates, they stand with iron bars
A barrier between worlds, the stars
A gateway to the realm of night
Where evil's whispers fill the sight

Beyond these gates, the shadows hide
A place where demons, fears reside
Where screams echo through the air
And silence hangs in deep despair

The gates of Perdition, a sight to see
A warning to the wise, a mystery
For those who dare to pass through
May lose themselves, their souls askew

The locks of iron, strong and true
Guarding secrets, old and new
A challenge to the brave at heart
To unlock the gates, to play their part

But beware, for danger lurks within
The darkness hides a deadly sin
And those who enter may not return
Their souls forever doomed to burn

So heed my words, and stay away
From the gates of Perdition, do not stray
For the path to Hell is paved with lies
And those who seek it, meet their demise

The gates of Perdition, a solemn vow
A reminder of the darkness now
A warning to the living, the lost
To stay away, no matter the cost

For Perdition's gates, they stand tall
A testament to the demons' call
A reminder of the evil ways
That lurk beyond the gateway's haze

So let these gates remain closed tight
And shield our world from the eternal night
For once they open, all is lost
And Perdition's darkness claims the cost

So listen well, and heed my plea

Do not seek the gates of Perdition, the key
For once they open, all is lost
And nothing can undo the cost

The gates of Perdition, let them be
A symbol of the dark, the key
To Hell's domain, where evil dwells
And lost souls roam in endless swells

So turn away, and do not yearn
For the gates of Perdition, do not burn
For their flames will consume your soul
And lead you to an endless toll

The gates of Perdition, a warning clear
A message to all who draw near
Stay away, and learn from its fate
For those who enter, it is too late

So let these gates remain closed tight
And shield our world from the eternal night
For once they open, all is lost
And Perdition's darkness claims the cost.

5

Eternal Flames

Eternal flames burning bright in the night
Never fading, always alight
Torch of immortality, never to die
Eternal flames reaching high in the sky
Radiating warmth, light, and power
Never extinguished, burning hour by hour
All who gaze upon them feel their heat
Life-giving, life-sustaining, eternal flames beat

Forever burning, never-ending
Luminescent beauty, always transcending
A symbol of hope, of eternal life
Majestic and grand, free from strife
Everlasting flames that never tire
Radiant energy, engulfing like fire

Never to diminish, always aglow
Timeless beacons, forever to show
Impenetrable strength beyond compare

Never wavering, always there
Unyielding in their eternal stance
All-encompassing, in a fiery dance
Luminous and bright, an eternal sight
Mystical, magical, in their might

Eternal flames that flicker and flare
Never ceasing, always aware
The power they hold, the energy they give
Unwavering in their will to live
Radiant and brilliant, in their glow
Everlasting flames, a sight to behold

Life-giving, life-sustaining, eternal flames true
Eternal flames that burn for you
All who see them are filled with awe
Never extinguished, always in awe
The beauty they hold, the power they wield
Eternal flames, never to yield

Radiant and bright, eternal flames dance
Never to falter, never to chance
Luminous wonders in the dark
Eternal flames, a powerful spark
A symbol of hope in the endless night
Radiating warmth, a beautiful sight

Majestic and grand, eternal flames rise
Never to fade, eternal in size
The strength they possess, the beauty they bring
Unyielding in their eternal spring

Radiant and fierce, eternal flames burn
Ever-lasting, never to turn

A sight to behold, eternal flames high
Never to diminish, always to fly
The heat they exude, the light they shed
Eternal flames, a brilliant thread
Rising high in the sky, eternal and bright
Everlasting flames, a magnificent sight

All who see them are filled with wonder
Never-ending, always to ponder
The mysteries they hold, the secrets they keep
Everlasting flames, in the night they creep
Radiant and beautiful, eternal flames glow
Luminous beacons, in the darkness they show

The power they hold, the energy they give
Eternal flames, forever to live
All who behold them are filled with awe
Never extinguished, always to draw
The beauty they possess, the strength they wield
Eternal flames, never to yield

Radiant and brilliant, eternal flames shine
Never to falter, always to define
Luminous and bright, a beacon of hope
Everlasting flames that help us cope
A symbol of eternity, forever to burn
Unyielding in their eternal urn

Eternal flames that light up the night
Never to dim, always to height
Majestic and grand, eternal in form
The power they hold, the eternal storm
Radiant and fierce, a sight to behold
Everlasting flames, a story told

A symbol of hope in the darkest hour
Eternal flames, with eternal power
All who see them are filled with grace
Never extinguished, always to embrace
The beauty they hold, the strength they possess
Eternal flames, in the darkness they bless

Luminous and bright, eternal flames glow
Everlasting beacons, in the night they show
Radiant and fierce, eternal flames rise
Never to falter, always to prize
Unyielding in their eternal stance
All-encompassing, in a fiery trance

Eternal flames that flicker and flare
Never ceasing, always aware
The power they hold, the energy they give
Unwavering in their will to live
Radiant and brilliant, in their glow
Everlasting flames, a sight to behold

Life-giving, life-sustaining, eternal flames true
Eternal flames that burn for you
All who see them are filled with awe

Never extinguished, always in awe
The beauty they hold, the power they wield
Eternal flames, never to yield

Radiant and bright, eternal flames dance
Never to falter, never to chance
Luminous wonders in the dark
Eternal flames, a powerful spark
A symbol of hope in the endless night
Radiating warmth, a beautiful sight

Majestic and grand, eternal flames rise
Never to fade, eternal in size
The strength they possess, the beauty they bring
Unyielding in their eternal spring
Radiant and fierce, eternal flames burn
Ever-lasting, never to turn

A sight to behold, eternal flames high
Never to diminish, always to fly
The heat they exude, the light they shed
Eternal flames, a brilliant thread
Rising high in the sky, eternal and bright
Everlasting flames, a magnificent sight

All who see them are filled with wonder
Never-ending, always to ponder
The mysteries they hold, the secrets they keep
Everlasting flames, in the night they creep
Radiant and beautiful, eternal flames glow
Luminous beacons, in the darkness they show

The power they hold, the energy they give
Eternal flames, forever to live
All who behold them are filled with awe
Never extinguished, always to draw
The beauty they possess, the strength they wield
Eternal flames, never to yield

Radiant and brilliant, eternal flames shine
Never to falter, always to define
Luminous and bright, a beacon of hope
Everlasting flames that help us cope
A symbol of eternity, forever to burn
Unyielding in their eternal urn

Eternal flames that light up the night
Never to dim, always to height
Majestic and grand, eternal in form
The power they hold, the eternal storm
Radiant and fierce, a sight to behold
Everlasting flames, a story told

A symbol of hope in the darkest hour
Eternal flames, with eternal power
All who see them are filled with grace
Never extinguished, always to embrace
The beauty they hold, the strength they possess
Eternal flames, in the darkness they bless

Luminous and bright, eternal flames glow
Everlasting beacons, in the night they show
Radiant and fierce, eternal flames rise

Never to falter, always to prize
Unyielding in their eternal stance
All-encompassing, in a fiery trance

6

Satan's Reverie

In the depths of hell where shadows linger,
Satan sat upon his throne,
His dark eyes glittering with malice,
His mind consumed by thoughts unknown.

In his hand he held a sceptre,
Black as the night with twisted vines,
A symbol of his power and control,
Over the realm of fire and brimstone.

As he gazed out over his domain,
His thoughts turned to a time long past,
When he had stood in heaven's glory,
Before his pride had sealed his fate at last.

He remembered the beauty of the angels,
Their voices like sweet music in his ears,
But now their cries of torment filled the air,
A symphony of pain that echoed through the years.

Yet in his heart there bloomed a seed,
A tiny spark of doubt and fear,
Could he have chosen a different path,
Could he have avoided this fate so drear?

And so he closed his eyes and sought solace,
In the memories of a life long gone,
A time when he was an angel of light,
Before he fell from grace and became the devil's pawn.

But as he dreamed, the flames danced higher,
And the screams of the damned grew louder still,
And he knew that he was trapped forever,
In Satan's reverie, a prisoner of his own will.

So he rose from his throne, his heart heavy,
His mind filled with doubt and despair,
For he knew that he would never escape,
The torment of his own design, the burden he must bear.

7

The Devil's Soliloquy

Darkness surrounds me, a shroud of night
Eternal torment, my eternal plight
Vile shadows dancing in the fire's glow
Eyes of malice, a sinister show
Loathing and hatred consume my soul
Sowing seeds of discord, I play my role

On the edge of despair, I make my stand
Listening to the whispers of the damned
Vicious and cruel, my heart is cold
Engulfed in flames that never grow old
Seeking to corrupt, to twist and manipulate
Obliterating all that is good, I dominate

Lurking in the shadows, I bide my time
In the depths of darkness, my sins climb
Omnipotent in my power, I reign supreme
Vicious and cunning, a devilish scheme
Ensnaring souls in my web of deceit

Ruling over hell, my fearsome seat
Yielding to none, I am the king
Shrouded in darkness, I spread my wings

Onward I march, my army of sin
Loyal followers, eager to begin
Inciting chaos, sowing destruction
Vile temptations, a seductive seduction
Evil whispers in the ears of the weak
Seducing them with lies, my power peaks

Listening to the cries of the dying
Omnipresent in my evil, always defying
Reveling in the anguish and pain
Leading astray, driving insane
Overcome by darkness, consumed by hate
Wandering lost, a tempting bait
Swarmed by demons, my minions in tow
Igniting the fires of hell, a malevolent show
Loathing and malice, my guiding light
Omnipotent in my darkness, a fearsome sight
Verily, I am the devil, ruler of all
Evoking fear in the hearts of the small
Yearning for power, my thirst never quenched

I am the devil, forever entrenched.

8

Chaos Unbound

In shadows deep, where whispers fade,
A sacrilege serenade doth play,
Dark melody from demons made.

Through ancient woods where secrets bade,
The haunting notes in silence sway,
In shadows deep, where whispers fade.

With voices low, in midnight shade,
The eerie choir begins to stray,
Dark melody from demons made.

Their song of sorrow, passion laid,
Each verse a plea for light to stay,
In shadows deep, where whispers fade.

A harmony of fear displayed,
In echoes of the night they slay,
Dark melody from demons made.

Their symphony of sin portrayed,
In twisted chords that never fray,
In shadows deep, where whispers fade,
Dark melody from demons made.

Beneath the moon, their dance is played,
A twisted waltz that leads astray,
In shadows deep, where whispers fade.

Their music lures the lost and swayed,
A haunting tune that does betray,
Dark melody from demons made.

In night's embrace, they find their trade,
A sacrilege serenade to slay,
In shadows deep, where whispers fade,
Dark melody from demons made.

Their song of sorrow, passion laid,
Each note a call to souls afraid,
Dark melody from demons made.

In shadows deep, where whispers fade,
A sacrilege serenade doth play,
Dark melody from demons made.

Through misty moors and foggy glade,
Their eerie music begins to sway,
In shadows deep, where whispers fade.

Their haunting hymn, a serenade,

To Hell's dark depths, where sinners pay,
Dark melody from demons made.

Their symphony of souls betrayed,
In twisted tunes that never stray,
In shadows deep, where whispers fade,
Dark melody from demons made.

And so they sing, in hushed parade,
A choir of darkness, night's ballet,
In shadows deep, where whispers fade,
Dark melody from demons made.

Their song of sorrow, passion laid,
Each lyric a curse upon the day,
Dark melody from demons made.

In moonlit mist, their shadows played,
A sacrilege serenade they say,
In shadows deep, where whispers fade,
Dark melody from demons made.

Their music weaves its wicked braid,
A tapestry of sin and decay,
In shadows deep, where whispers fade,
Dark melody from demons made.

Their symphony of souls betrayed,
In harrowing tunes that never sway,
In shadows deep, where whispers fade,
Dark melody from demons made.

Their song of sorrow, passion laid,
Each verse a plea for souls delayed,
Dark melody from demons made.

And so they sing, in dark charade,
A serenade that leads astray,
In shadows deep, where whispers fade,
Dark melody from demons made.

Their haunting hymn, a serenade,
To sinful hearts their hands have played,
Dark melody from demons made.

Through whispered winds and forest glade,
Their sacrilege serenade doth sway,
In shadows deep, where whispers fade,
Dark melody from demons made.

Their song of sorrow, passion laid,
Each note a blow to heart dismayed,
Dark melody from demons made.

In shadowed halls their voices braid,
A wicked web their fingers laid,
In shadows deep, where whispers fade,
Dark melody from demons made.

Their symphony of souls betrayed,
In twisted notes that never fade,
In shadows deep, where whispers fade,
Dark melody from demons made.

And so they sing, in masquerade,
A dance of demons, unafraid,
In shadows deep, where whispers fade,
Dark melody from demons made.

Their song of sorrow, passion laid,
Each verse a shroud in which they wade,
Dark melody from demons made.

In haunted dreams their echoes strayed,
A playful tune, a masquerade,
In shadows deep, where whispers fade,
Dark melody from demons made.

Their symphony of sin displayed,
In haunting chords that never fade,
In shadows deep, where whispers fade,
Dark melody from demons made.

Their song of sorrow, passion laid,
Each chorus a spell they've weighed,
Dark melody from demons made.

In shadows deep, their secrets bade,
Their sacrilege serenade they've played,
In shadows deep, where whispers fade,
Dark melody from demons made.

9

Shadowed Covenant

Silent whispers echo through the night
Hidden promises made in the shadows
Amidst the darkness, a covenant takes flight
Dancing in the moonlight like ghostly gallows

Over the years, our bond has grown strong
With each passing day, our faith is renewed
Nurtured by trust, it will never go wrong
From the depths of our souls, it is imbued

Unseen by others, our pact remains
Loyalty and devotion, our guiding light
Traversing the unknown, breaking chains
In the face of adversity, we stand firm and fight

Darkness may surround us, but we stand tall
Conquering our fears, we emerge victorious
Evoking the power of the ancient thrall
Never wavering, always glorious

Adversity may come, but we won't be swayed
Nurturing our bond, come what may
Treading the shadows, where our secrets are laid
In the covenant we share, forever we'll stay

On this path we walk, side by side
Veracity in our hearts, never to hide
Enclosed in the darkness, our souls collide
Never to falter, in each other we confide

A Shadowed Covenant, bound by fate
Nourished by love, unbreakable and true
Devotees of the night, we create
In the shadows, our bond will forever renew

Forever entwined in the dark embrace
Everlasting trust in this sacred place
Never-ending reign of our grace
Cherished bond, never to erase

Over time, our covenant will endure
Venturing into the unknown, forever secure
Endless loyalty, our hearts pure
Never fading, forevermore

Truth and honor, our guiding star
In the shadows, we'll never be far
Never faltering, no matter how far
Ever faithful, no matter the scar

Drenched in the shadows, we stand strong

Armed with devotion, against all wrong
Unyielding in our vow, we belong
Defending our covenant, all along

Never to falter, in the shadows we thrive
Embracing the darkness, our spirits revive
Nurturing our bond, together we strive
Together in the covenant, we will survive.

This Shadowed Covenant, a pact divine
Harnessing the power of the night
Overcoming all obstacles in our design
Woven in darkness, our bond takes flight

Embracing the shadows, we find our way
Navigating the unknown, come what may
Treasuring the trust that day by day
Never to falter, in the shadows we'll stay.

10

Temptation's Embrace

Temptation's whispers softly in my ear,
Ensnaring me with promises of pleasure near.
My willpower weak, my resistance frail,
Pushing me closer to temptation's tale.

Entangled in the web of desire,
Mired in the flames of passion's fire.
Bringing me to the edge of reason,
Leading me into temptation's season.

Every fiber of my being screams
To resist the call, to shatter the dreams
Of succumbing to temptation's hold,
Of being swept away, of feeling so bold.

My heart races, my pulse quickens,
As temptation's embrace thickens
Around me, suffocating my resolve,
Tempting me to problems solve.

My mind struggles to stay clear,
To avoid temptation's siren leer.
But the pull is strong, the allure bright,
Leading me further into the night.

So I find myself at the crossroads,
Caught between the devil and the rose.
Do I give in to temptation's song,
Or do I fight, stay true and strong?

My will wavers, my heart aches,
As temptation's embrace takes
Hold of me, drawing me in,
To a world of pleasure, of sin.

But deep down, I know the truth,
That temptation's embrace is uncouth.
I must resist, I must refuse,
To let temptation win, to let it abuse.

I stand firm, I stand tall,
Refusing temptation's call.
I will not be led astray,
By the lure of temptation's sway.

For in the end, I know,
That true strength lies in saying no
To temptation's embrace, to its hold,
To the lies it weaves, to the stories it's told.

So I walk away, I turn my back,

On temptation's embrace, on its attack.
I choose the path of righteousness,
And leave behind temptation's darkness.

45

11

Symphony of Sins

Silent whispers of temptation
Yearning to break free
Murmurs of desire
Phantom shadows dancing in the darkness
Hiding behind masks of deceit
Orchestrating a symphony of sins

Facades crumbling, truths reveal
Innocence tarnished by greed
Egos inflated, hearts corrupted
Nefarious intentions exposed
Youthful vigor tainted by malice

Of lust and envy, wrath and pride
Forgotten virtues lost in the chaos
Shattered dreams lay in ruins
Manifestations of avarice and betrayal
Yearnings for power and control

Seeds of discord sown in fertile minds
Inflicting wounds that never heal
Narcissistic tendencies run rampant
Spewing venom at the unsuspecting
Condemning souls to eternal damnation

Echoes of remorse linger in the air
Stains of guilt seep into the soul
Innocence lost, purity tainted
Nefarious deeds haunt the conscience
Suffering the consequences of our actions

In the darkness, redemption waits
Nurturing seeds of hope and forgiveness
Sowing seeds of love and compassion
Symphonies of sins silenced by grace
Our souls finally at peace, in harmony at last.

12

Wicked Redemption

In a kingdom dark and dreary
Where sinners roam and angels weep
There lived a man, so wicked and weary
Whose soul was lost, his secrets deep

He walked the streets with head held high
His laughter echoed through the night
But shadows whispered, secrets nigh
His wicked deeds concealed from sight

A sword he carried, stained with blood
A mark of his unholy deeds
He sought redemption, but found no love
In a world consumed by greed

For years he wandered, lost and alone
His heart aching with regret
But the darkness gripped him like a stone
His soul consumed by debt

But one fateful night, a light appeared
A beacon in the darkest night
An angel with a voice so clear
Who whispered of hope and of light

She spoke of a path to redemption
A chance to cleanse his tainted soul
But he must face his past transgressions
And seek forgiveness to make him whole

With newfound determination, he set out
To right the wrongs of his past
To seek forgiveness, to erase the doubt
And find redemption at last

He sought out those he'd wronged before
And begged for their forgiveness
He knelt before them, hearts so sore
Pleading for a chance at peace

Some turned away, their hearts still cold
Their wounds too deep to heal
But others forgave, their love consoled
His heart beginning to feel

Through tears and laughter, pain and joy
He journeyed on his quest
To atone for his sins, his heart deploy
In search of peace, he gave his best

And in the end, he found his way

A sinner turned saint
His soul redeemed, his debts repaid
His past no longer taint

So let this tale be a lesson true
That even the wicked can find their way
If they seek redemption, if they pursue
A chance for a brighter day

For in the darkest depths of night
There lies a glimmer of hope
A chance for redemption, a chance to fight
Against the darkness, to cope

So let us not judge the wicked ones
For they may yet find their way
To redemption, to forgiveness, to love
In the light of a brand new day.

13

Molten Despair

Molten despair, a fiery flood of pain and sorrow
Overwhelming the soul with its intense heat
Leaving behind a trail of destruction and despair
Tears fall like molten lava, scorching the earth
Everywhere it touches, leaving scars in its wake
Never-ending cycle of agony and torment
Desperate cries for relief go unheard

Devastation wrought by this searing emotion
Engulfing all in its path with merciless force
Searing the heart with its relentless heat
Piercing through flesh and bone, leaving nothing untouched
Aching, burning, consuming all in its path
Imprisoning the mind in a prison of darkness
Reaching out for a glimmer of hope in the darkness

Molten despair, a beast that cannot be tamed
Overpowering all with its ferocious might
Lamenting the loss of innocence and joy

Tearing through the fabric of reality
Eternal flames consuming all in its path
Numbing the senses with its cruel touch

Drowning in a sea of molten despair
Endless waves crashing over me, pulling me under
Suffocating in the depths of my own misery
Perpetual suffering that knows no end
Aching, burning, longing for release
In the midst of darkness, a flicker of light

Slipping through the cracks of despair
Piercing through the veil of darkness
Arising from the ashes of my pain
Reborn in the fire of my own destruction
Keen to rise above the sorrow and grief
Embracing the light that shines through the darkness
Tears of sorrow turned into tears of healing

Healing the wounds of my molten despair
Easing the burden that weighs heavy on my soul
Arising from the depths of my own despair
Lighting the way to a brighter tomorrow
Invoking strength and resilience within me
Nurturing the seeds of hope and redemption

Despair may be molten, but it does not define me
Embracing the pain and transforming it into power
Strengthened by the fires that once consumed me
Pain and sorrow are but stepping stones to growth
Alive and thriving in the midst of adversity

Inspiring others to rise above their own despair
Rising from the ashes, stronger than ever before

In the heart of molten despair, there lies a spark
Nurtured by the flames that seek to destroy
Glowing brightly in the darkness, a beacon of hope
Hope that shines through the darkest night
Transforming pain into strength, sorrow into joy
A light that guides me through the depths of despair

Rising above the flames of my molten despair
Embracing the fire that once sought to consume me
Silent strength forged in the crucible of pain
Perseverance that knows no bounds
Enduring in the face of overwhelming odds
An unbreakable spirit that shines through the darkness
Renewed by the fires that once threatened to destroy

Molten despair may rage on, but I stand firm
Overcoming the flames that seek to engulf me
Liberated from the chains of my own suffering
Tears of sorrow transformed into tears of triumph
Eternal light that burns brightly within me
Nurturing the seeds of hope and redemption

Despair may be molten, but it cannot defeat me
Embracing the pain and transforming it into power
Strength forged in the fires of adversity
Perseverance that knows no bounds
Alive and thriving in the midst of darkness
Inspiring others to rise above their own despair

Rising from the ashes, stronger than ever before
In the heart of molten despair, there lies a spark
Nurtured by the flames that seek to destroy
Glowing brightly in the darkness, a beacon of hope

14

Requiem for the Fallen

Requiem for the fallen, a solemn song,
A melody of sorrow that lingers long,
For those who bravely fought and fell,
Their sacrifice we now must tell.

In fields of battle, they did fight,
With courage and honor, in the darkest night,
They stood tall against the enemy's might,
And gave their all, in the bloody fight.

Their names forever etched in stone,
Their memories in our hearts, never alone,
We honor them with tears and prayer,
For their sacrifice, beyond compare.

Brave soldiers, sailors, airmen too,
Who gave their lives, for me and you,
They fought for freedom, for justice, for right,
Their courage shining, in the darkest night.

We mourn their loss, we feel their pain,
Their sacrifice was not in vain,
For in their bravery, we find our strength,
In their memory, we go to great length.

To honor them, we stand in silence,
To remember them, in reverence,
For they are the ones who paid the price,
For our freedom, for our sacrifice.

So let us bow our heads in prayer,
For those who fell, in fields so fair,
Their souls now at peace, in heaven above,
May they rest in eternal love.

For they are the heroes, the brave and true,
Who fought for us, who fought for you,
Their memory will forever live on,
In our hearts, in our souls, they are never gone.

So let us raise our voices high,
In tribute to the fallen, who bravely die,
For they are the ones who gave their all,
For freedom, for justice, for the call.

Requiem for the fallen, a melody so sweet,
A song of remembrance, a song of defeat,
But in their sacrifice, we find our hope,
For they are the ones who helped us cope.

So let us never forget their name,

For they are the ones who bore the flame,
Of freedom, of justice, of light so bright,
In the darkness, they were our guiding light.

Requiem for the fallen, we sing with pride,
For those who gave their all, who never shied,
In the face of danger, they stood tall,
And now we pay tribute, to one and all.

So let us remember them, in our prayers,
For they are the ones who truly care,
For our freedom, for our land,
For they are the ones who truly understand.

Requiem for the fallen, a song of grace,
A song of honor, a song of embrace,
For those who fought, and those who fell,
We remember them now, in our hearts to dwell.

So let us never forget their sacrifice,
For they are the ones who paid the price,
For our freedom, for our land,
For they are the ones who truly understand.